DAVID
MOYES

STEVE
WATSON

Everton

NIGEL
MARTYN

JAMES
BEATTIE

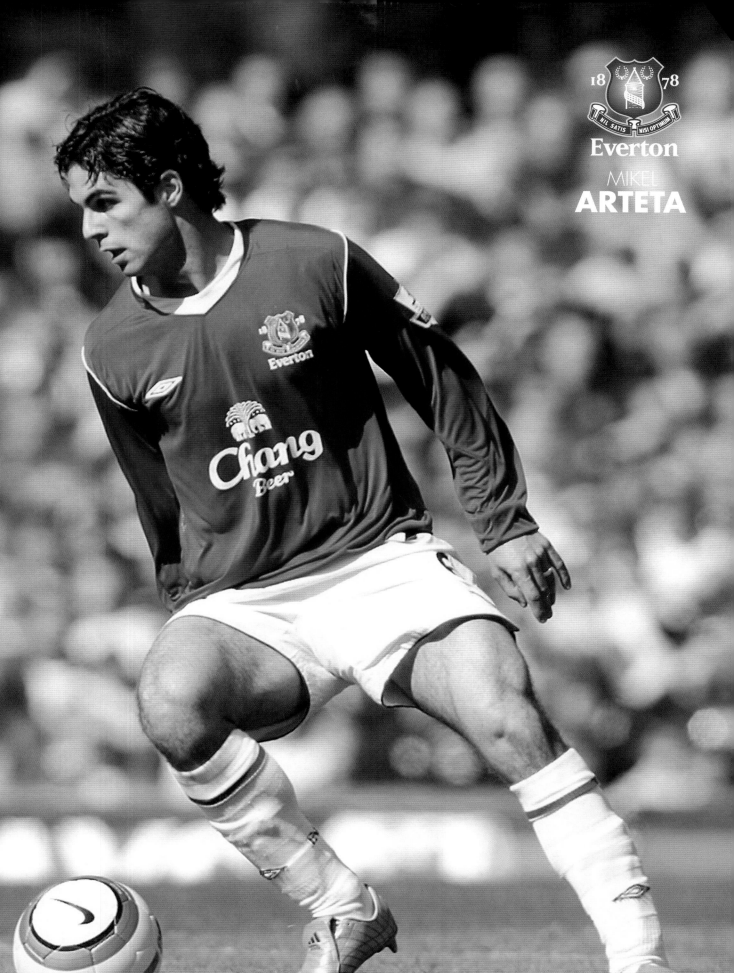

Everton

ALAN
IRVINE

JOSEPH
YOBO

Everton

KEVIN
KILBANE

DAVID MOYES

MANAGER OF THE SEASON

Everton

18 78

Everton

MIL SATIS NISI OPTIMVM

TIM **CAHILL**

Everton

THE PEOPLE'S CLUB

Everton

MARCUS
BENT

Everton

THE ART OF
CELEBRATING

LEON
OSMAN

LEE
CARSLEY

Everton

DUNCAN
FERGUSON

Everton

ALESSANDRO
PISTONE

James
McFADDEN
Everton

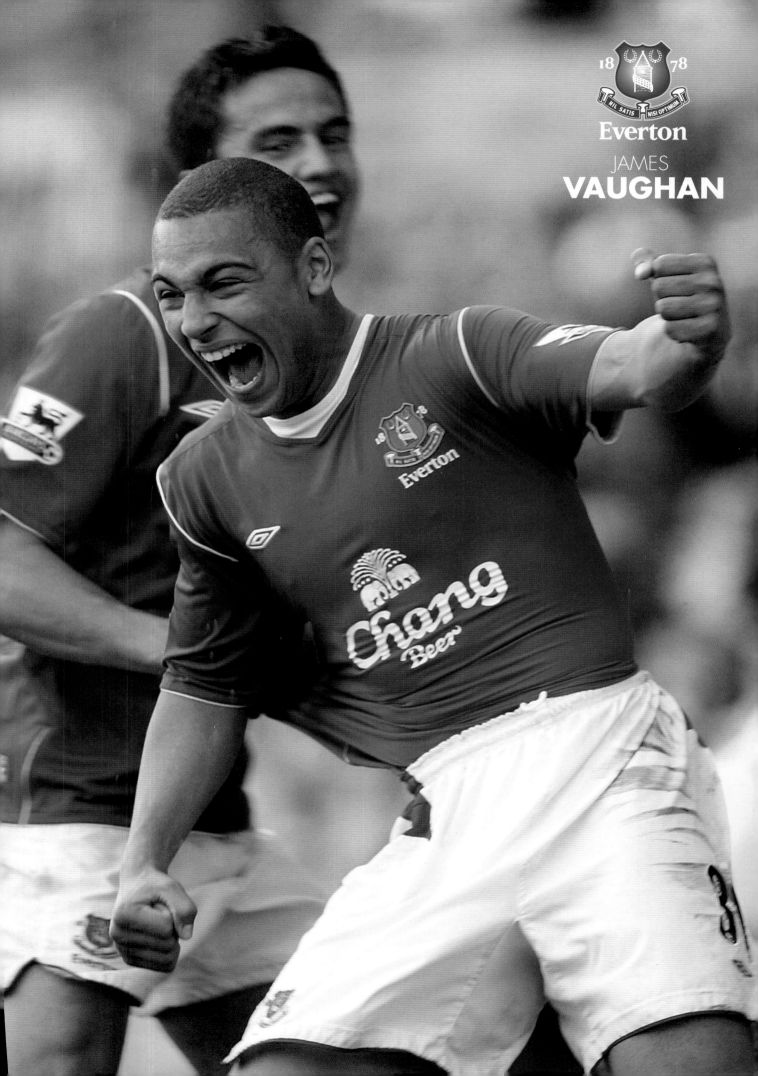

James
VAUGHAN

Everton

GARY
NAYSMITH

DAVID
MOYES
ALAN
IRVINE

AWAY THE LADS
2004-2005

ALL TOGETHER NOW

Everton